CRAZY MONEY

THE TRUE COST OF MENTAL HEALTH

Written by Bliss McIntosh Green

Self Help/Finance/Money

Published by

Passionate Pathways

8738 Arbor Creek Drive Ste. B

Charlotte NC 28269

Send request and feedback to guidedbybliss@gmail.com

Name: Green, Bliss McIntosh, author

Title: Crazy Money the True Cost of Mental Health/Bliss McIntosh Green

ISBN:978-1-7351545-2-7

Library of Congress Control Number: 202291942

This book is dedicated to those who struggle but have hope.

Crazy Money

The True Cost of Mental Health

Our sanity is precious, but it is often managed at the highest expense. When we look at why we make choices and decisions financially; our feelings are to blame. Our feelings are warehoused in our psyche. When we have a great head space, we make awesome choices! When we are in mental and emotional chaos.... who knows how this plays out? The same is true for our finances.

There are a few things that must occur to create harmonious spaces of synergy between crazy, money, and our peace.
We must develop a relationship with our finances/money
We must identify how crazy we are, and how it shows up in our money
We must invest in our money and ourselves. Practice self-

care and get professional
help.
We must earn in every way
possible
We must educate, protect,
and preserve our funds

Crazy can be managed.
Money can be managed.
Mental wellness can be
managed. We get to choose
what we want and what we
will allow.

Emotionally Abused

"Could you be a narcissist that is gas lighting your money in more ways than one?" -Bliss Green

The average person has a silent lover/friend. Many of us go around ignoring them and just dragging them along at our pleasure and whim. We disregard and disrespect them often. We deplete their value at every opportunity. We tell ourselves lies and justify the way we treat them. When they leave us, we are shocked and sad. We don't know how to really exist without them, so they come back to rescue us. We replay this terrible psychotic toxic dysfunctional cycle repeatedly.

This lover/friend is ignored and taken for granted and it wants us to acknowledge it, make time for it and respect it. This silent lover is called MONEY. When I say MONEY, I mean all things financial. Our money is often emotionally abused.

headspace. So now that we've established that the average person is crazy... let's get some CRAZY progression and results!

Make it simple

"Life is really simple, but we insist on making it complicated." – Confucius

You could say that our relationship with our finances is more complicated than need be. At any stage of our lives our relationship with money is one of 3 things

UP--Happy Healthy, Secure and Growing
DOWN--Burnt Out, Stagnant, or Depressed
DYING—Toxic or Traumatized

Clearly, we always want to be UP. We want to feel our best and have optimal finances. The reality of life is there will be times that we don't feel good. My money may hit a downward economic cycle. We must always focus on moving forward. We look upward and focus on elevation.

There have been times where I was depressed, burn out,

and inactive. My money reflected these energies too. Life goes from 0-100 in complication in 0.5 seconds.

It's not that we will never hit lulls or lows, we will.
It's the momentum we create to press on and move forward that determines how long and how often we experience the dips in life. We must find a way to make things simple.

I have a

Forgiving
Undesired
Tragedy
Uplifting
Renewing
Energy

When my emotions start to go stale, or begin to slow, I pull out my affirmation and manifestation tools. I focus on the future I am creating. Once we define our head space, we give clarity to present circumstance and momentum for our future. A healthy functional relationship with money allows us to have a future. This acronym is also a powerful anger management solution. #ihaveafuture

Forgiveness

"To err is human to forgive is divine"

When I think of this quote I literally think, "Only God could do this...to forgive". Forgiveness is one of the most difficult things in life to do because it requires understanding and acceptance at the same time.

There are things we don't understand, but we must accept. There are things we accept that we will never understand.

Most often the hardest person we must forgive in any circumstance is ourselves. Forgiveness is one of the most powerful resources we possess that allows us to move past our emotional pain/trauma. It allows us to channel our intentions to a higher place and purpose. When we forgive, we are not excusing the past, we are no longer allowing the past any power over our present or future.

When we do not forgive, we create undesired emotions that build up in our head space. Eventually we find a way to balance them or compensate for them. We then literally spend money to make ourselves feel better. I'm not saying this is a bad thing. I'm asking, what if we could just forgive? How much money could we save, then invest, then accumulate for a life to be LIVED?

Take some time each day to forgive yourself, and consider showing some grace to others, even if they don't deserve it. The yields and dividends on forgiveness are exponential. Your future self will thank you.

Undesired Tragedy

The most annoying things happen to the coolest of people.

We must not allow the undesired aspects of our lives to trap us into victimhood. When we allow life to weigh us down, we start slowing down. Its super hard to stay depressed when you are active, involved, and on purpose with your missions and goals in life. Life is distracting. Depression and distractions are a trap that will lead you to an undesired place.

Being a sitting duck in life is surely a target for tragedy. Terrible things happen to innocent and amazing people. Tragic experiences often create trauma and paralysis in our emotional world. Circumstances may not be our fault, but our lives are our responsibility to survive, improve, and live with joy.

We must propel ourselves forward and upward, no matter how much pain, numbness, or inconvenience we experience.

Uplifting Renewing Energy

"Life, liberty, and the pursuit of happiness"
I love this quote because it suggests that one may not be happy, but it's a worthwhile pursuit.
If we did everything based on how we feel in life, very little would get accomplished. We must act on facts and faith. Both what we know, and the optimism of our future beliefs.

For us to do this, we must experience freedom.
Freedom from our emotional triggers and pain.
Freedom from our bad habits and past decisions.
Freedom from doubt and limiting beliefs.
The only way to become free, it to unlock the renewing energies. We are a series of vibrations. The more self-awareness we possess, the more love, healing, and

abundance we can create. These resources are renewing energies that manifest what it is we desire in life. Money is an energy, and the more we practice renewing our energy, we can learn to magnetize and multiply our money.

You have a future. We have a future. No matter what has occurred in our present or our past, we can pivot to the beauty we are creating, and

arrive in those moments securely and safely.
Teach this mind over matter technique to your family.
Hope is such a powerful tool to bring about a beautiful future. #ihaveafuture
It will help them release anger and create freedom.
Rome wasn't built in a day, but over time, you will construct a better place that you built on emotionally sound principles. Find a way

to develop better relationships in your life, especially with money. Make it simple.

Crazy Money

"Too many people spend money they haven't earned, to buy things they don't need, to impress people they don't like." – Will Smith

You can be crazy and have money
You can have crazy money
You can be crazy about your money.
You can neglect your money, and just be crazy!

Let's acknowledge that our common denominator is that WE ARE ALL CRAZY. Each of us gets to choose how crazy, what crazy, when crazy, and who gets to see this crazy. 😊 If one must be crazy, please have money. It's the best kind of crazy to be.

People **who are crazy and have money** are what we call abnormally- normal. These are just ordinary folks adulting every day. Most people fall in this category. "Just a little crazy" is controlling a lot of wallets. Now you see why our society is completely hypnotized by consumerism. The good news is that this level of crazy is manageable, and high functioning. Controlling our mental narratives internally and externally allows us to control our emotions and our finances to a positive outcome. We create stability, joy, and inner peace at this frequency of life. We can live our best lives and prepare for our future. When we are crazy with money, we can figure out how to focus and get SUPER CRAZY...in a good way!

People **who have crazy money** are called wealthy. If we are all crazy, we should all aspire to this level of craziness! Having crazy money is permanent financial security, and all the pleasures that this life can afford. Talk about crazy good, right? When you have crazy money, you can afford to manage your mind. You can afford mental and emotional therapy. You can hire the best medical care, a maid, an assistant, a personal trainer, a chef, a massage therapist, a psychologist, a life coach, and a driver (for those of us who experience road rage)

They say, “insanity is doing the same thing over and over again, expecting a different result.” As you progress your crazy good or bad... make sure you are managing your mind. Get your emotions/mindset the professional support it deserves.

History and statistics teach us that there is a thin line between genius and psychosis. So, the question is, are we crazy enough? Will we continue to do what is known and comfortable or will we do the thing that makes us learn and grow? Will we cower away from our dreams when others don't understand our assignment/journey? Having money is not everything, but we all know that money covers a multitude of problems in life. The more financial security we can create, the better we will feel about our future. The better we feel about ourselves, the better we can manage our emotions, and the emotions of others.

FACT

Emotional Stability is the gateway to financial security.

People **who are crazy about their money** are obsessed. Don't allow your "securing the bag" force you to lose the **#lifeofbliss**

There is a proverb that states," The love of money is the route of all evil" Money itself is an energy. It is a means to an end. When we make a good thing become a bad thing because of GREED, then we often loose our sense of direction. When we lose our priorities and direction, we find ourselves in unintended locations and circumstances.

Greed can create blurred lines. Becoming obsessed with accumulating wealth, can lead to short cuts and toxic relationships. (Up to and including imprisonment) This is CRAZY bad. This is exactly why the mind MUST be managed. "A mind is a terrible thing to waste", and if you let your mindset and emotions go unchecked, they will lead you down a path that is CRAZY HORRIBLE!

When we **chase** money, we convert it from an energy to an object. We then begin to hoard it. We define it as scarce and finite. When we ***attract*** money and allow it to flow to us and through us, we keep the frequency of abundance. We allow money to remain an energy. The energy is not confined to access or limitations. It is limitless and infinite.

Our internal compass must always point north. Our north star is what we want most in life. It is our WHY. When we stay positioned “north facing”, we will always know what direction to take, and we can easily know when we are led astray.

In our lives, “liberty and pursuit of happiness”, we must remember to keep the main thing the main thing. Money always takes care of itself when we learn to respect and take care of it. We must keep the balance and the rhythm of life as we achieve crazy good things!

People who neglect money are just crazy!

We can do way too much (obsessions) We can do way too little. (neglect) This is the worst crazy you could be. When we don't prioritize our money, we are bound to experience financial loss. Staying mindful and remaining self-aware is a gateway to saving money and accumulating wealth. This requires us to pay attention.

What are you feeling?

Our emotional triggers can force us to ignore warning signs of drama/trauma.

Where is the money flowing to?
Services and fees all cost us money each month that we never think to consider. We practice mindless and reckless spending all the time. Financial Institutions are always "nickel and diming" us to low liquidity. Retailers are

always baiting us and manipulating our self-esteem/ego to spend our money. Overcompensating for emotional losses drains us financially and emotionally.

Living within your means. This phrase means get a plan and stick to it, or as I like to call it, The Budget.
The good news is there is help and hope for us all. We can get professional therapy. We

can reduce stress and anxiety. We can make healthy choices and decisions. Whatever we do, make sure we deal with the crazy we are, and secure the $money bag$!

Love Yourself

"<u>You are a Badass</u>" - Jen Sincero

The correlation between mental health and money is jaw dropping.

When our emotions are in control of our spending, terrible things can occur.

Jealousy purchases for keeping up with the Jones'

Angry purchases for self-validation or gratification

Depressed Purchases for lifting us out of a mood

Toxic Purchases to help us forget our pain.

The quickest way to tell if you love yourself is to look at your finances. Fully loving ourselves requires us to love our past, present, and FUTURE. There's no clearer way to demonstrate this self-love than to monitor and increase our savings accounts AND investments.

This is not about how much you have, but *do you* have

assets/accounts and are you working on contributing to them?

When we talk about physical and emotional self-love, we are describing the actions and outcomes of self-reflection, peace, abundance, and stability. Our choices and decisions reflect these attributes. These attributes pay dividends. The opposite is true. When we don't love ourselves, we look for ways to fill voids, enable toxic people and behaviors, and drain resources in pursuit of happiness. When self-love is distant, we feel insecure and drama prone.

Our self-esteem plays a vital role in our financial security. If we don't believe we are worthy of love, then we develop the self-fulfilling prophesy that love is hard and will evade us. As we develop a relationship with our finances on an intimate level, we discover our core values and belief system is overriding all that we wish and hope for. Are we worthy of our dreams? Do we believe that financial security is in our immediate future? Do we deserve to be independently wealthy? Are these things that happen to others, or are these things that are happening to us? We must first believe. We must Love

Ourselves and allow ourselves to win.

Do you know what your core values and emotional triggers are?

We may not even understand why we are compelled to make the choices we do. The way we feel about ourselves is often a reflection of the way we feel about the world.

Doing the personal development and training your self-esteem is a huge step in financial recovery and developing a healthy relationship with your money. Not to mention the physical and mental aspects of abundance and prosperity. Love Yourself, be better to yourself and your relationship with money.

Self Esteem is key. Believe you are worth the investment

in yourself. Believe you are worth your dreams. Believe your life has purpose. Believe you are extraordinary! Doing the shadow work is so important. Resolving issues, creating new patterns and identities is so essential. People see what occurs in the sunshine, but your life is what show's up in the shadows.

Go to therapy, or even create your therapy. Whatever you

do, get help so you can live the life you deserve. You are worth your dreams, but you are also the one denying access to them. Love Yourself, because as Jen Sincero says, you are a Badass!

Delayed Gratification

"The ability to discipline yourself to delay gratification in the short term in order to enjoy greater rewards in the long term, is the indispensable prerequisite for success." – Brian Tracy

The amount of thought that is required to plan for a "future rainy date" is intense. Consider the discipline and sacrifice that is required to achieve the greater good. Delayed gratification is something that winners thrive on. To win later, you must wager the delay of gratification. This is how you develop the trust between yourself and your money persona. Delayed Gratification. Are you willing to wait for the rewards of long-term commitment?

Savings is the greatest delayed gratification. Savings saves lives. Watching your bank account stack is the highest level of adulting possible. Creating a financial security blanket allows you to sleep more peacefully at night. Sweet Gratification in due time. Save, Save, and Save some more.

Investments are a game changer. It's looking at your money and saying," I'm so serious about you, I'm taking us to the next level..." Investments are a multiplier. You can't earn your way to wealth. You can't save your way to wealth. You can invest your way to wealth. If you want true intimacy with your money, save and invest. It requires concentration and time. It requires a plan. You must put in the work. It is delayed gratification. Your future self will thank you.

You get to choose how you save and invest.
You can use fixed assets, variable assets, real estate, or block chain technologies. The possibilities are endless. Get

started saving and investing today.

The Price of Pride

"Pride goeth before destruction and a haughty spirit before a fall." – Proverbs 16:18

Denial is deception. We all need help. There is no shame is getting help. As a matter of fact, it's CRAZY not to see a healthcare provider if you are feeling feelings and thinking thoughts that are consuming you.

We need to normalize therapy. We need to advocate for it. Being a friend is realizing the "record is broken and on repeat" and telling our friends that they need talk with a therapist to get back to the feel-good music.

In my youth, I wish my friends would have told me this. I was traumatized and angry. Even now, with therapies, I still experience anger, just less expressive. 😊 I've learned that its ok to be angry. It's not ok to let your anger dominate your actions, reactions, and relationships. For decades my family and friends endured the toxicity of my pent-up anger, and masquerading pain. I needed help unpacking my layers. Help that my loved ones could not provide.

My pride prevented me from having a lot of wonderful things. Irony, I thought my ego was protecting me with denial. There are so many excuses to hold onto a pain party blanket.

Everybody is angry right? I mean anger is a natural emotion to feel. I'm just human.

I'm not physically violent! Those people are out of control and need help.

Who has money for therapy?
I'm doing my best to make it and just be at peace.

Eventually, I discovered just how costly my anger, pride, and denial were. My masked anger has cost me relationships. My overcompensating for pain, has ruined precious relationships. Over time, my fuses ran low. I lost filters and decorum, and even some professional relationships. Profitable relationships.

For a long time, I felt that not being ok, was not ok. I spent most of my life hiding the trauma of my father's addiction, our financial fragility, and being expected to press onward. I felt seeking professional assistance felt awkward and made me feel that I was weak.

I was weak. I was breaking and withering away, bit by bit, and didn't even know it. I thought that only people who were out of control need therapy.

I was out of control, so much so, that I desperately desired to control everything I could. Especially people. Not so much in my work life, but in my personal private life. So much so, that I'd get angrier when I received an unintended outcome. I was edgy and discontented. I was sad and unhappy, and my name is Bliss for God's sakes. My luggage of anger wrapped in pride was a heavy load, that I traveled with for a long time.

We are all travelers, but we learn to pack light. The silver lining to my story is that with a lot of prayer, trial and error, therapy, self-discovery, education, and common sense, physical activities, and grounding, I learned that my goal was not perfection, but surrender.

There are not perfect people, only perfect moments. Accomplishment is the result of planning, but things seldom occur according to our plans.

Control is an illusion, and a deception of masking feelings about self-worth.
When we Surrender to the right people and the process of life, we experience the freedom of knowing joy, pleasure, and peace.
Today is for grace and forgiveness.
Tomorrow is for new thoughts, behaviors, and abundance.

Every day I am LOVED (Living One Valued Experience Daily) Every day I have a FUTURE (Forgiving Undesired Tragedy Uplifting Renewing Energy) I am BLISS (Believing Life is Something Special)

Today I am emotionally stronger, and much more profitable. Today, I have savings, which has saved my life over and over. Today I have investments. Today I am experiencing abundance. Those of you who are judging me, I hope you reflect on your fingers pointed to you. Those of you who know this pain.... There is hope and more abundance for us all.

360° PAID

"Get Money" - Junior Mafia

Can you have a conversation about wealth and not talk about income? To be specific, incomes. (plural)
It is a firm belief of mine that one of the biggest ways we have failed our youth is by not sharing that fact that it takes multiple JOBS, INCOMES, people contributing to make it and get ahead.
Whether people inherit money, earn money, or magnetically acquire it, we

must look for ways to make receiving income a multidimensional practice.

We must learn to layer and stack our incomes so that we have money coming in every direction of our lives.

There are so many modules on how to get paid.

I like to think of this as

My Job- Trading time and talent for money

My Investments- Recurring Income

My Opportunities—Things I create that create money for me

My Systems—Tools I utilize that make money while I sleep

An example for this would be
My assets increase in value. (Real estate and digital assets)
My podcast develops a community of like-minded people who want to create financial security via real estate.
My books are a marketing tool and an income stream
My online courses educate people on the process of becoming better qualified for getting approved for a home loan.
My merchandise is a monetized manifestation of all these things that are possible, while I "say it with my chest."

All these tools help people to find me, save people time and money, and allow borrowers to #ownhouses and #closewithbliss because I'm a mortgage loan officer. #mortgagegal #lendingbliss 😊

The moral of my story is the more money I receive or earn, the easier it is for me to save, invest, and #ownhouses. I personally want to create financial security, and live the life I choose, on my terms. You can too! #Ucan2

We each have a superpower. Even if we have not yet

identified our strengths, we can take our interest and perfect them into marketable skill sets. Therefore, education and exposure are so important.

There are endless opportunities for us to make money, and we should consider as many as are congruent with the amazing lifestyle we desire to lead. Feeding into the expectations of others will keep us lacking.

We are without the abundance we desire. Society will tell you there is one right way to do things. Only do one thing at a time.

Who made society the end all wealth oracles? You can do more than one thing at a time. You can find a way to have multiple streams of income. The key is to do what makes the most sense to you. What gives you the greatest return with the least amount of effort? Your income needs leverage. Don't stop with just one source of income. Keep working until you can financially insulate your life from undesired and tragic events. This is financial freedom and security. This is world peace. The piece of the world that you own and control.

Educate
Protect
Preserve

"Buy, Borrow, Die "- What the rich say

No matter where we come from, we learn how to perceive the world. We are taught by our family and our culture how to form opinions and pre-judgements. This is where our limitations reside. As we age, we gain exposure and experience which shapes/alters our world view. This determines if our world is possible, or impossible. Education teaches us to question if the world is in fact flat.

We must experience education so we can concrete our core beliefs or destroy them. Education is where theory meets application. Change will never occur without action or application. As we take inventory of our mindset and our core beliefs about money and our mental stability. We must remember to learn from our past and develop our expectations of our future. We must teach others to do the same. The great news about money is the only person that can tell you how to obtain it, cultivate it, and share it, is yourself. You must seek it out. You must request the infinite wisdom of its acquisition and preservation.

Remember to educate yourself on how to increase

your wealth, and always prioritize your health. “To whom much is given, much is required” is a proverb that sums up life and lending. When you are in possession of something, you must take precaution to preserve said asset.

We must protect and preserve our incomes.

We must protect and
preserve our
investment/savings
We must protect and
preserve our credit
We must protect and
preserve our peace of mind.

Do you Overstand what it
means to take ownership?
When we take ownership of
our money and real estate,
we must learn the
responsibility of ownership

and how to get the best results for our assets.

What does protection look like?
You may have life insurance, or managed asset accounts. Insurance is one of the best ways to ensure protection from losses. Over time, be sure to update your information with the asset company.

Do you have estate planning? Fortunes are lost to poor estate planning. You've worked hard to provide and leave a legacy. Don't let it die in taxes, and litigation due to avoidance of your certain demise. (death) Plan ahead and choose how your legacy lives on. Get a will. Consider a Trust. Hire the attorney. Your future generations will thank you.

Priceless Peace

"Your Peace is priceless." – Manisha Mishra

The cost of mental health can be astronomical when you total sum all that we do to obtain peace. Peace is precious. Peace is priceless.

The internal battle we must all face is managing our physical and mental health while creating financial stability. This is easier said than done. Life hits us very hard and unexpectedly. As we experience transitions, we discover just how crazy and reactive we are.

Let's tell the truth. We spend money to AVOID pain or CREATE pleasure. Maybe at the same time.

Something is sucking our time and money.

Self-Medicating- Our Addictions – Drugs, Sex, Alcohol, Gambling

Self-Distracting- Our Obsessions – Hobbies, Collections, Social Media, TV, Streaming Programming

Obligations and Priorities- Our friends and family

The only way to get to the root cause of our pain is to allow it to be felt.

Get alone and get silent. Turn off all devices and remove all distraction. Learn how to slowly practice meditating.

Quiet your racing thoughts that you spend most of your time silencing. Listen to these thoughts. Feel your feelings. Write your feelings. Write your feelings until you understand them. Give your feelings a positive outlet (that doesn't involve spending money, or self-destructive behavior) Seek professional therapy if you are consumed by your feelings and thoughts.

Its ok to not be ok. Its ok to be angry. Its ok to be overwhelmed and confused. Its ok to feel unsuccessful. Its ok to start over. Its ok to advocate for yourself. Its ok to create boundaries. Its ok to acknowledge you are not happy and not feeling well. Its ok to feel numb.

Numb and net neutral is a safe space to be. Learn to get there and stay there. If you are always racing to feel happy and doing everything in the world to avoid feeling down or depressed, you need to seek professional help. For you, it may be more than just "mind over matter", it may be a chemical imbalance.

There is a direct correlation between crazy, money, and our peace. For us to find our stability path, we must do the following

- We must develop a relationship with our finances/money
- We must identify how crazy we are, and how it shows up in our money
- We must invest in our money and ourselves. Practice self-care and get professional help.

- We must earn in every way possible
- We must educate, protect, and preserve our funds

The better we become at managing our minds, the faster we can manifest world peace and the finances to enjoy it.

If you are struggling with your physical or mental health, please know there is hope. There are people who genuinely care about your future and well-being. Please take every opportunity to live your life on your terms, in a positive manner. Know that everyday will not feel good. On the days you don't feel good about yourself, take the time to discover the root cause of your feelings and unpack those emotions. I like to do the following things to protect my peace.

Write a journal entry. It helps to get your thoughts out on paper.

Walk and talk. I recite affirmations of validation and determination as I walk.

Pray. Some call this meditation. Concentrate on the future you want while giving yourself grace for the present you are experiencing.

Celebrate loving yourself and doing the "next best thing" this can be small acts and or large ones.

It is so important to practice self-love. It is the very center of finding peace. The absence of peace of mind is the beginning of chaos, and an expensive path to financial ruin.

Prosperity

"The strongest single factor in prosperity consciousness is self-esteem: believing you can do it, believing you deserve it, and believing you will get it." -Jerry Gillies

When we think of prosperity, most think money. However, I’d conclude that the beginning and end of prosperity is peace. Prosperity is a peace sandwich.

Peace

Health

Financial Security

Pleasure

Peace

The beginning of all solutions is gratitude. Being thankful for where we are and where we are headed is so important. It is the catalyst by which miracles occur. Start with gratitude and create peace.

There is a direct correlation to our mental health and our money. If we desire a better relationship with money, we must first assess our mindset, and our emotions. The more we get to facts over feelings, the better we will manage our relationship with our finances. The better relationship we build with money, the better we can create the perfect peace sandwich by which we shall find great satisfaction and security.

The goal is never to compare, but to surrender to your best. Where there is peace, you'll discover a fountain of profitability. It's crazy to imagine what a wonderful world this could be. You'd be crazy not to create the best life you can experience for yourself and others! Be this crazy!!!! Create peace, your personal world peace.

I am wishing you exponential abundance, "peace which passeth understanding", and that your WILDEST dreams come true.

I am rejoicing for your future & that the craziest money is generationally sustaining you!

Written By:
Bliss McIntosh Green 2022

Abundance Always & Shalom

If you or someone you know is suffering, help is available. The ultimate cost of an unhealthy mind is the loss of life. If you are having thoughts of harming yourself,

please call the suicide
prevention hotline at

800-273-8255

Made in the USA
Monee, IL
04 November 2026

67375802R00066